Just as the journey
of a thousand miles
starts with one step

So does the beginning
of a magnificent quilt
start with one stitch

On the cover

Title: Unknown
             The design is a reflection of Kamakani Ka Ni Aloha, ca. 1900 and Garden of
             Kauai, ca. 1910.

Quilter: Unknown. Made in Maui for a family who lived in Kalaupapa, Molokai

Date: ca. 1923/1925

Owner: Quilts Hawaii
             Special mahalo to Leone Kamana Okamura of Quilts Hawaii in Honolulu for
             providing the quilt for the cover of this book.

HAWAIIAN QUILTING MADE EASY

First Printing, February 1997
Second Printing, February 1999
Third Printing, March 2001
Fourth Printing, January 2004
Fifth Printing, May 2006
5 6 7 8 9

ISBN-10: 1-56647-195-8
ISBN-13: 978-1-56647-195-4

Mutual Publishing, LLC
1215 Center Street, Suite 210
Honolulu, Hawaii 96816
Ph: (808) 732-1709
Fax: (808) 734-4094
e-mail: mutual@mutualpublishing.com
www.mutualpublishing.com

Printed in Taiwan

TABLE OF CONTENTS

Here are two examples of early Hawaiian quilts. Notice the Missionaries' patchwork influence on the first quilt. The bottom quilt is of the Hawaiian Lily Pattern. Photos courtesy Archives.

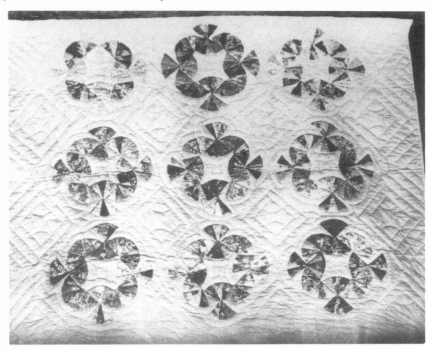

A LITTLE ON THE HISTORY OF QUILTING IN HAWAII

"Monday morning, April 3rd, the first sewing circle was formed that the sun ever looked down upon in this Hawaiian realm. Kalakua, queen dowager, was directress. She requested all the seven white ladies to take seats with them on the mats, on the deck of the Thaddeus." So were the words written by Lucy G. Thurston in her diary describing the arrival of the first Missionaries to Hawaii in 1820.

After 18,000 miles and 163 days from Boston, the brig Thaddeus was anchored off the northern coast of the island of Hawaii at Kawaihae. Kawaihae, at that time, was a very popular port. The area is now more widely known for the outstanding Mauna Kea Beach Hotel. The ship's Captain had sent a scouting troupe ashore, which came back announcing the death of King Kamehameha the Great and that his eldest son, Liholiho, would be crowned Kamehameha II.

On the eve of April 2nd an invitation was sent ashore inviting the principal chiefs to come aboard. Kalanomoku, Prime Minister of the King, was first aboard, followed by Queen dowager Kalakua, her sister Queen Namahana and two wives of Kalanimoku. Interestingly enough, Kalakua had brought a web of white cambric to have a dress made in the fashion of the day, and was very particular about having it finished before they arrived in Kailua, then the capitol of Hawaii.

On the morning of April 3rd, Mesdames Bingham, Thurston, Holman, Whitney, Loomis, Ruggles and Chamberlain sat on the deck of the Thaddeus and started teaching the four Hawaiian ladies their first sewing lesson, using calico patchwork. The New England ladies had much experience in making quilts of intricate designs from scraps of material leftover from the complicated dresses of the 1820s. It was only natural that they would want to share this feminine talent with the ladies of their new land using scraps of material brought with them from Boston.

Stella M. Jones in her book on Hawaiian quilting makes several references to quilts of the olden days, including one made by Princess Pauahi of elaborate and beautiful silk patchwork, and another made by young Hawaiian girls from the Lima Kokua Society in Hawaii presented to the Bingham family. This excellent book republished in 1973 is available in book stores and in your public library and should be a must for anyone seriously interested in Hawaiian quilting. It includes over 75 pictures of quilts. In 1830 Mrs. Laura Fish Judd received a friendship quilt from New England where each block had an outline stitch of quotations from the Bible, and signed by the donor.

While reference is always made to the first sewing circle being held on April 3, 1820, someone did a little sewing before the Missionaries came, because the tapa robes were sewed with olona fiber; sails were sewn using a bone needle and sennet rope; and many of the higher chiefs' wives did wear free flowing dresses. But undoubtedly, the Missionaries did teach the Hawaiians how to quilt, and increase their sewing skills.

For those curious about the status of the white cambric - the dress indeed was finished for the arrival in Kailua, and Kalakua, who had embarked with 4 layers of tapa in a pau from the waist down, covered with a loose dress, debarked in an ankle-length white gown, wearing a white lace cap with a wreath of roses, and a half lace hankerchief with a corner "enhanced by an elegant sprig of various colors". Hundreds of greeters along the shore shouted with glee when she debarked.

No one knows exactly when or where the Hawaiian quilt, as we think of it today, was started. The Hawaiian quilt, unlike the patchwork and straight lines of sewing introduced by the Missionaries, follows the contour of the pattern over and over in tiny stitches, making the cloth ripple like the waves or the wind. The most popular belief is that it probably began evolving in the year 1858 when a prince was born to the king - the first in over 50 years. Many women made covers as a gift for the infant.

Whatever the beginning, it was, and is, a beautiful art that reflects the profound creativity & beauty of the Hawaiian soul. Quilt patterns are usually assigned names. Usually they are named for what they represent: flowers like ginger, plumeria, lilies -- or trees like breadfruit or palms. Other more complicated designs carry a bigger theme such as "Garden Island", "The Beauty of Maui" or a very popular theme "My beloved flag".

There are many versions of the creation of the Hawaiian quilt, several related in Stella Jones' book. One mother was nursing her child thru an illness and while dozing beside the bed one night, had a vision of a quilt design, which later became clearer - so clear in fact she decided to make it, finishing the quilt thru her daughter's convalescence, and giving it to her as a gift. Still another version tells of Leilani, a young Hawaiian girl who fell in love with a Chinese man, but was forbidden to marry him. Although the mother finally condescended she would not allow her daughter to have any of the quilts or calabashes as heirlooms. When Leilani arrived in Honolulu she was ashamed of not having a cover for their bed, and ashamed to ask for a pattern. One night, she too had a dream - a dream so vivid she got up and cut the pattern directly out of the material, basted it on the background and went back to sleep. When she awoke in the morning, she was so pleased, she started quilting with the help of a friend, and named the quilt Ka La'i o Pua (The calm of Pua Lane). Still another story tells of a lady drying her sheets under a breadfruit tree, and the rays of the sun etched a pattern on the sheet. The lady thought it was so attractive she decided to make it into a quilt pattern.

It is customary to write the name of the quilt along the seam on the wrong side of the background material. It is also customary to sign your quilt, either as a special design in the center of the quilt, or along one of the corners.

CHAPTER 2 - SUPPLIES

Many a quilt's been made with just needle, some thread, and the material, so don't let a long list of "supplies" bother you. The following list is given with the thought there may be some new things on the market that helps make quilting easier.

A. QUILTING HOOP   These come in various sizes. Buy the one that fits your need best. If you're going to do a lot of quilting, there's even a square one that comes on an adjustable stand. The Islands do not have as good a supply as on the Mainland, but the Sears mail order catalog has an excellent assortment.

B. SHARP PINS: Ordinary straight pins, preferably silk pins, will do, but there are special quilting pins on the market, longer than ordinary pins.

C. BEESWAX:

D. NEEDLES: Use a No. 8 or 9 (betweens) quilting needle for quilting. A quilting needle should be short and strong for going thru 3 layers of fabric. A thinner needle is better for appliqueing, and a much longer needle works easier for basting. Remember - the larger the number, the shorter the needle.

E. ART GUM: Excellent for removing spots and light penciled lines.

F. SCISSORS: Use your own choice, but make sure they are SHARP. Some are made special to go thru 2 or more thicknesses.

G. DRITZ MARKER: This is an excellent tool for making contour lines. You simply follow the last line stitched on the point of the marker, and the chalk makes a line exactly the same at whatever distance you want to quilt.

H. RULER:

The Dritz Marker has a 6" ruler (in centimeters too). However, a regular 12" ruler, or even a yardstick on large projects, comes in handy.

I. THIMBLES:

Some quilters prefer two. One for the middle finger (pushing finger) of the quilting hand, the other a half thimble for the thumb. Fancy thimbles, such as China, will not work as they have no grooves. Look for deep grooves when you are buying thimbles for quilting. There's an excellent thimble on the market by one Carol Bradley, gold plated at about $14.00 with deep grooves, and a puka (hole) on the top for your fingernail to protrude.

J. THREAD:

There's a special quilting thread, stronger and not as twisty as regular polyester dual duty, but it is limited in shades. The regular polyester dual duty is satisfactory but works better if it is run over beeswax, taking care not to overdo with the beeswax. Some teachers advise using thread the same color as your material, while other's recommend a contrasting thread which shows greater contrast. However, the contrasting thread makes errors or uneven stitches easier to note. Always thread needle as it comes off the spool. This reduces twisting.

K. SEAM RIPPER:

An excellent tool when you want to remove a few stitches.

L. PENS & PENCILS:

An ordinary lead pencil is satisfactory for marking patterns if you use a light line. The new Wonder Marker is very satisfactory. See complete discussion on page 9 for marking materials.

CHAPTER 3 - MATERIAL

Use only the best. If you are going to spend months creating an heirloom, it should be done on fabric that will last for years. Percale with a tight even weave is best and broadcloth, also with a tight weave is next. However, modern day polyester and synthetics are not to be overlooked. Elizabeth Akana, teacher at the Bishop Museum, and an expert quilter, first started working on polyester and thinks it is easy. Quilters who have always worked on cotton think a polyester blend is evasive and slippery. Silks and velvets have often been worked into beautiful quilting projects.

PREWASHING: Most fabrics of today do not need prewashing. If you are in doubt, ask the clerk when buying material.

BATTING: A bonded polyester is best. It comes by the yard in different "weights" which actually mean thickness. There is also a type that comes in packages of specific sizes. Do not buy "Fiberfill" for batting as this is all soft material, the type used for stuffing. What weight is best? A matter of personal preference. Heavier weights have more loft. Also, heavy fabrics need a heavier batting.

AMOUNT OF MATERIAL NEEDED: Will depend on your project. Small projects - pot holders, table mats, appliance covers can sometimes be made of scraps, or a yard of material goes a long way on small projects. Pillows - material depends on size. Two, 22 inch pillows may be made from 1½ yards of contrasting colors. A double or queen size bed will take nine yards of 44" material, each in Back, Front & Applique.

Most of these fabrics come in 44" or 45" widths, so you may want to design your project to a size that would have minimum waste. The material for the applique, background and backing should always be the same, to avoid problems in future washing. There are exceptions after you become a more experienced quilter.

MARKING THE MATERIAL:

Complicated patterns for appliqueing need to be drawn on the fabric before cutting. These lines are not important, because they will be turned under or stitched over. However, lines that are marked to help with the quilting should be easily removed.

A test was made on 100% yellow cotton percale, drawing lines with a lead pencil, tailor's chalk in red, white & blue, dressmaker's pencils in white and blue, carbon paper in red and blue, and the Wonder Marker. The Wonder Marker and white chalk came out with a simple rinse in plain cold water. The other had to be scrubbed with soap & brush to come out, and the red carbon placed with a tracing wheel never did come out.

You are cautioned to ALWAYS test all markers on a scrap of material you are using. For example, the Wonder Marker carries a warning not to launder with soap before rinsing in plain water, because some soaps cause the marks to turn brown.

Experienced quilters rarely mark contour, or echo lines, on their quilts, but most beginners find it difficult to follow straight lines or even contour lines without marking. The Dritz "Tai-lor-ette" listed previously, is a wonderful gadget for drawing contour lines. Just follow the last quilted contour line with the protruding point, set the chalk point for the space of your next contour line, and a perfectly even line will be drawn.

CHAPTER 4 - DESIGN

The designs of Hawaiian quilts have always carried very special meanings, and it is hoped you too will create some lovely designs reflecting your feelings of Hawaii. The flowers and trees have been repeated many times. as have patterns commemorating special occasions. If you do trace a design from a flower or leaf, cut it first on a paper pattern, and turn under a hem as would be required in appliqueing. You will probably find you want to redo the pattern a little larger! See the pattern traced from nature on page 42.

PATTERN ETHICS IN THE OLD DAYS - In Stella Jones' excellent book "Hawaiian Quilts" as originally written in 1930, and as republished in 1973 by the Daughters of Hawaii, the Honolulu Academy of Arts and the Mission Houses Museum, several paragraphs are devoted to a fairly well-defined code of ethics on the use of quilt designs or patterns. With permission of the Honolulu Academy of Arts, this is the way Ms. Jones explains it:

> "The originator of a design names it, and that design and that name are held inseparable. Exchange of patterns has always been held a bond of close friendship. While another to whom the pattern has been given can alter the design to suit her taste, introducing new elements and changing the proportions, the name prevails so long as the general outline is retained. Color can be changed without thought, though some designs naturally imply the use of certain colors.
>
> Patterns have been known to have been stolen even from the clothesline where the quilts had been hung to dry or to air, for some women, very clever with scissors, could stand far off and cut the pattern by sight. The originator of a particularly well-loved pattern wisely kept it secret until the coverlet was quilted, thereby establishing her undisputable claim.
>
> The owner of a design, upon finding it strayed from home, might compose a song slyly making reference to it, which would greatly embarrass the stealer. It is well, therefore, in cutting a pattern obtained surreptitiously to alter the design sufficiently to make a brave claim for originality."

Every true lover of Hawaiian quilts should pay a visit to the sleepy little town of Waianae on the northwest coast of Oahu. The Waianae library has over 400 quilt patterns and over a hundred pillow patterns, which you are allowed to trace. The No. 52 Makaha bus will drop you off practically at their front door. It's a wonderful library and a wonderful staff. Unfortunately, they wouldn't allow me to include one of the patterns in this book.

The size of design will, of course, vary with your project. Be careful when using 'store bought' patterns that they fit your needs. When given thought beforehand, it is easy to shorten or lengthen a pattern. That is why throughout this book, you are urgently requested to make a complete pattern on paper before cutting your material.

When drawing your own designs - the following chart may help:

Length of pattern on bias	Material needed for applique	Paper to cut pattern (fold into triangle)	Open bias size will be	Open straight size will be
7"	10" sq.	5" sq.	14"	10"
8"	11½ "	5 3/4 "	16"	11½"
9"	13 "	6 1/2 "	18"	13"
10"	14 "	7 "	20"	14"

Extra tips: When drawing a design on newspaper, a colored pen is easier to see.

You needn't be too fussy. A line 〰 will turn under ——

Draw a design - any design - starting with a 3½'' straight line, which will be placed on the bias when you are ready to cut your trial design. This size is recommended, since the design can be cut from a seven-inch square, and the entire project from one 8½ x 11 sheet of paper.

Here is a sample:

Make sure this portion is on the straight fold!

Your pattern will look like this

CHAPTER 5 - CUTTING A DESIGN TO APPLIQUE

Many patterns are included in this book, and you are encouraged to use them "as is", alter, or merely as a guide for creating your own. When selecting a pattern for a particular project, carefully measure your pattern to be appliqued. This is why it is so heavily emphasized to always cut a full size paper pattern and lay it on your background material before cutting your fabric. It is so easy to make the pattern a little smaller or larger. This is somewhat redundant from the previous chapter, but it is so important it bears repeating.

Appliques may be cut from one flat piece of material, such as the hibiscus used on the pot holder, or a double fold such as that used on the pineapple explained on page 19. On these simple designs, it is not necessary to draw the pattern on the material, but you may if you wish. However, you can cut around the pattern which has been pinned to the fabric. In the case of the double fold, put extra pins on the material, outside of the pattern, as the material slips easily.

FOLDING THE FABRIC FOR AN EIGHT-FOLD CUT

On making the four and eight-folds, much more care is necessary, and again you are urged to make a test pattern on paper. If working on a pillow, a brown shopping bag makes a good pattern, and good for your test cut of the entire pattern. If working on a larger project, a newspaper or tracing paper will do, but these will have to be pieced and taped together. Try making simple designs on the eight-fold of small piece of paper until you get the feel of it.

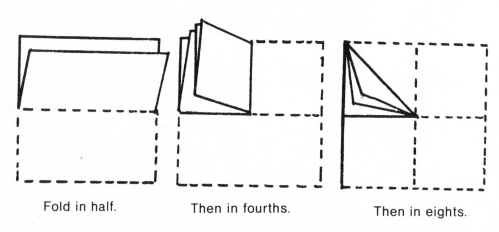

Fold in half.   Then in fourths.   Then in eights.

As you complete the above folds, press firmly after each fold. After you make the last fold (creating the triangle) be very careful to check your folds and points, making sure they are even, and press again. Press both the applique material and the background material. **The place where all the folds meet in a point is the center of your pattern.** Many quilters like to make a small design in this center point.

Double check your fabric to make sure the bottom line from the bias is all on the double fold. If there are any single layers of paper (or fabric) you have folded wrong. For example, if you make the last fold from top left to bottom right (instead of as in the illustration) your applique will not come out in one piece! Many a beginner has cut a pattern only to find it came out in pieces instead of one piece.

PIN PATTERN TO FABRIC

Carefully pin the pattern in place through all eight thicknesses. Be generous in using pins. Put pins in the fabric outside of the pattern too. Just 1/16th of an inch slip will distort your pattern.

Carefully draw around pattern on your material. Remove pattern, replacing each pin through all eight layers of fabric as they are removed from the pattern. Cut carefully with very sharp scissors. Leave the material folded until you are ready to pin and thread baste the applique on the background material.

Look how two 'snips' will change your pattern!

Snip

Snip

CHAPTER 6 - BASTING

BASTING THE APPLIQUE

Remember the emphasis put on pressing the 8 folds of material firmly? These folds are used as a guide when placing applique on background material. It is important to be sure the line on the bias cut is on the bias line of the background material, and the straight lines of the applique are on the straight lines of the background material.

1. Always start in the center, by pin basting.
2. When thread basting, never baste close to edges. About ½ inch inside design is suggested.

The above directions may sound simple, but they are exceedingly important. If you start basting in one corner, your pattern will become easily distorted. First baste the center, then baste out to each corner, filling in with basting as required for your pattern.

The caution "never to baste close to edges" is because you want to be able to turn edges under for appliqueing without removing any basting stitches. The distance you will baste from edge will actually depend on how much you turn under, but ½ inch is a good rule. When basting thin leaves or stems, merely run a basting stitch up the center, not going to the point as it will be turned down.

BASTING FOR QUILTING

Take your time basting. It is time well spent. Basting for quilting is much different than basting for appliqueing. When working with three layers of material it has a great tendency to slip.

Assemble your project on a large flat surface where you can conveniently work. Backing should be first, then the filler, and the appliqued piece on top, right side up. When adding the filler, if it is necessary to piece, do not overlap but lay side by side and stitch seams together; otherwise it will separate.

Pin baste, the center, the four corners and a few points inbetween. Do not use too many pins, as they pull the material too tight. Always thread baste soon after pin basting, using a white basting thread. Some quilters prefer using a color of a sharp contrast for basting, but sometimes the colors bleed onto the fabric, particularly if left for a long period of time. It's easier to baste using a much longer needle than that used for quilting.

Remove pins as you thread baste and constantly check the back, smoothing it as you sew. You will have lots of puckers on the back, if you aren't careful. It is not necessary to make knots while basting although some people prefer to.

Quilts are handled differently since they are so large. Place backing on a flat surface, with seams up. Tape corners and centers of edges with masking tape. Most quilters do this on the floor. Next add batting, being sure to stitch over edges of batting where they are joined together. As said before - do not overlap, but lay side by side. (Seams will separate if not stitched and you will have flat areas in your quilt.) Next add appliqued material, top side up, matching edges to backing, and again tape with masking tape.

Now you are ready to start basting these three layers of material together.

CHAPTER 7 - APPLIQUEING

Appliqueing starts with your three basic steps:

1. Pin baste
2. Threat baste
3. Always start appliqueing in the center.

There are three basic stitches for appliqueing. The blind stitch and hem stitch, where you make the stitches as invisible as possible, and the overcasting stitch where you stitch down thru the fabric, underneath the applique, and come out on the top side at the edge of the applique. There is also a fourth method decorative stitching, which comes more under the category of embroidering than appliqueing. Appliqueing is also frequently done on the machine. This is not considered an authentic way to create Hawaiian quilting, although yearly more and more innovative methods are added to Hawaiian quilting. The fine stiches made so lovingly by classic Hawaiian Tutus is indicative of their easy way of life with no thought of going zoom-zoom-zoom- on a sewing machine.

HOW MUCH TO TURN UNDER?

The amount of material you turn under will be a matter of personal preference, your pattern and the material. If you turn under a small amount, like 1/16th inch, it is very important to make close stitches, otherwise it will fray. If working on fabrics that fray easily, you must take more than 1/16th inch. If you turn under more like ¼ inch, it is harder to go around curves and you lose a lot of your design. Also, if turning under ¼ inch, it may be necessary to clip, particularly at curves. A word of warning - If you do clip, do not clip completely to the turn-under-line. Perhaps 1/8 inch would be a happy medium.

NEEDLES FOR APPLIQUEING

It is easier to work with a thinner needle for appliqueing than quilting. It goes thru the fabric easier. Sharps No. 7 or 8 are fine.

CURVES AND POINTS WILL GIVE YOU THE MOST PROBLEM

If you aren't experienced at quilting - have patience. Even professional quilters often pay to have their quilts appliqued! Curves and points will give you the most problem. Remember - just one stitch at a time, and don't try to turn under more than just a little in front of your needle. The percale fabrics react nicely to finger pressing and it will stay in place. When approaching outer points, keep turning under as for straight lines, then turn point down approx. 1/8 inch. Continue appliqueing completely to the top. Then turn over the left hand side, making a perfect tip without a problem. Start appliqueing down the opposite side. For inner points, stitch very close to inner point, using your needle to help turn material under. At the inner point, make very close stitches, (practically like a satin stitch), until you are able to turn under the other side. See sketches on next page.

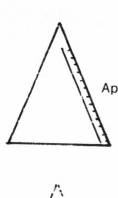 Applique within a short distance of point

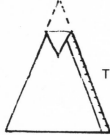 Turn tip down and continue appliqueing to point

 Turn opposite side under and continue appliqueing

 Make very close stitches at inside curve. You won't be turning under as much material here

 Sometimes in appliqueing round designs it is helpful to clip. Do not clip to turn-under-line

CHAPTER 8 - QUILTING TECHNIQUES

Hawaiian quilting follows the basic techniques of all other quilting with emphasis on three points:

1. Usually just two colors are used.
2. The quilting stitch is repeated in even rows around the contour of the design, making a rippling or echoing effect.
3. Instead of small patches, the typical Hawaiian quilt design is all cut from one piece.

Large quilts, in the old days, were made on frames especially designed for this purpose. Frames of this type are still being used at quilting demonstrations. Most quilters of today use a large hoop such as that pictured with the list of supplies. For smaller projects, use a smaller hoop.

Hoops come in many sizes and shapes, including oval and square. Many quilters feel the oval hoop does not hold the fabric as taut as the round hoop. There are even hoops on adjustable stands. All hoops are easily tightened to keep the material taut for even quilting.

There is another school of thought that believes quilting can be done without the use of a hoop. Again quoting Elizabeth Akana. "I used that method of quilting as you go, because I was always on the go and could carry a small pillow project in my purse. Once I started using a hoop, I found I had more control of my stitiches. I prefer the smaller, more even stitches I get with a hoop, and now carry my applique projects in my purse".

In an interesting book "QUICK AND EASY QUILTING" *by Bonnie Leman, she writes about people discovering quilting can be done very satisfactorily by holding the quilt in the lap, without a hoop. With her permission, here is how Bonnie describes "lap quilting".

> In lap quilting the stitching procedure is somewhat different than in frame quilting. When the quilt is stretched taut in a frame, most (not all) expert quilters use two motions to make each tiny stitch. The right hand rests on top of the quilt, the left hand is placed below it. With the right hand the needle is pushed straight down thru-all layers; it is then pushed straight back up with the left hand. Anywhere from six to fourteen stitches per inch should be taken in this manner, the number depending on the skill and experience of the quilter. When the quilt is allowed to fall loosely in the lap, the needle should be passed in and out in a single movement. This allows the cloth to hump upward a little above the needle, which produces the slightly rippled effect characteristic of quilting. The hands assume the same sewing position as when a running stitch is to be taken in a single layer of cloth. Only one or two stitches at a time should be taken in order to keep the stitches short and of uniform length. The number of stitches per inch is usually from five to nine, depending on the thickness of the fabrics and filler as well as the experience of the quilter."

> *quoted from QUICK AND EASY QUILTING by Bonnie Leman, published by Moon Over the Mountain Publishing Co., 6700 W. 44th Ave., Wheatridge, Colo. 80033 $6.95.

START QUILTING IN THE CENTER

A very important part of quilting is the very first row of stitching right next to the design, on the background material. It should be as close as possible to the edge of the design. This helps give a three dimensional effect. The quilting needle, as mentioned under supplies, should be a short sturdy needle easily pushed thru the fabric. A number 7 to 9 (quilting or between) needle is recommended. It is approximately one inch long.

To start quilting, a single knot is made on the end of the thread last off the spool, and the first stitch is made from back to front, pulling the knot thru the backing with a little tug, leaving the knot in the batting. The little hole in the back will disappear.

Some insist that a quilting stitch is not a running stitch; that it is straight up and down. While it is true the down stitch should be made down as straight as possible, the return stitch coming up from the back cannot be straight up if you are making 2 or 3 stitches. Whatever you call it, the straighter you make the first down stitch in each grouping, the easier it is to make small stitches.

When working on a large project, many quilters have several threaded needles going at the same time. It makes it easier to keep the same tension over a wider area. Whether you sew from right to left, or left or right is a matter of personal preference, but do keep the stitches going in the same direction for the entire project.

NUMBER OF STITICHES PER INCH

This is another controversial question. More important than the number of stitches is the evenness. Making even stitches should be your goal, and it is easy to control the length of the stitch of the front as you come thru from the back. Most quilters agree that 5 or 6 per inch is a goodly amount. When you read about 10 to 12 stitches per inch, they are usually counting back and front stitches. There is really no point in making your stitches as tight as a machine stitch. Each time you make a stitch, be sure you go thru all three layers of material.

When finishing your thread, the most popular method is to stitch back over the last 2 or 3 stitches then a large stitch or two in the batting, pulling the thread thru to the back and clipping.

QUILTING EDGES

When quilting edges or corners, it will be necessary to move your hoop beyond the material. To keep the material taut, add a strip of material between hoop and three places in the pillow, pinning thru all three layers of material. In the middle one strip will do. At the corners, two strips will be necessary per the illustration to the right.

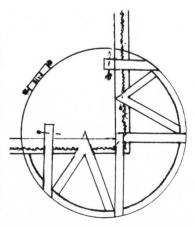

Mrs. Serrao, who specializes in pillows, uses a wooden frame made by her husband, the correct size of her pillows. The quilting is attached with eight pieces of elastic, thus never having to move until the pillow is completely quilted.

CHAPTER 9 - LET'S START WITH A POT HOLDER

The size can be anything of your choice. We have used 6 pieces of material, 9" x 6". The batting should be cut a little larger, so it will be in the binding. We have also used two designs - one to practice straight lines, the other to practice contour lines. The pineapple lets you practice cutting on a one-fold material, and the hibiscus is cut from unfolded material. You may use the Pineapple Pillow pattern by placing on a fold, rather than the 8-fold.

On the first pot holder, (pineapple) we used one layer of batting which did not make a satisfactory holder for really hot pans. On the second (hibiscus) we used two layers of batting, which was much better. There is an excellent product on the market called "Thermalam" made specifically for heat resistent projects. Some people also use old mattress pads or towels for lining pot holders.

Pin baste   Thread baste

1. First cut pattern.
2. Pin Baste.
3. Thread baste center, then about ½ inch in from the edge. In the case of the pineapple, baste up each leaf in the center.
4. Applique, using a blind or applique stitch.
5. Arrange backing, batting and appliqued design on top. Pin baste, then thread baste.
6. Start quilting in center, then quilt around the design, on the background, as close to the design as possible. Continue quilting using straight lines for the pineapple, contour lines for the hibiscus, following the illustration page 20 or create your own design.
7. Be sure to add a magnet or loop before finishing the binding.

In the center illustration, (b) there are at least 6 quilting mistakes. See if you can find them.

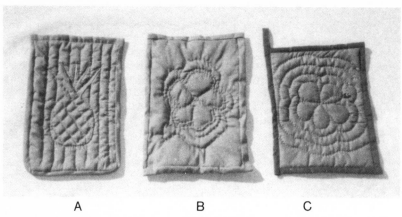

A   B   C

Errors on B.

1. There should be no quilting at edge of yellow applique. 2. The first line of quilting around applique on the background is too far from pattern. 3. Quilting stitches are inconsistent length. 4. Contours are inconsistent width. 5. Contour lines made too close allow for no puffing or loft. 6. An oblong design would have been better on the oblong background. 7. Quilting STOPS in the middle of nowhere.

HIBISCUS PATTERN FOR POT HOLDER. The pineapple Pattern is that used for making pillow A on page 23, cutting it on one fold instead of an eight-fold.

Add a special touch
of embroidery
if you like.

CHAPTER 10 - THE HAWAIIAN PILLOW

Pillow forms come in every size and shape imaginable. Or perhaps you have a pillow you want to recover. Whatever the size you decide to make, determine the required yardage based on using 44" material - which is the most common for percale and broadcloth. If anything should happen that your quilted cover does not fit the exact pillow planned, you can always fill it with shredded foam available loose by the bag, or "fiberfill".

Our instructions will be for two 18" pillows. You will need one yard of one color and a half yard of a contrasting color. You will also need two 18" squares of muslin for backing. (Old sheets would do.) You may mix and match the applique vs. the background in any manner you choose. Here is how to layout the material for cutting. These cuts will give you more strips for binding than you need — but it will give you a chance to use contrasting binding, or the same color binding as background material.

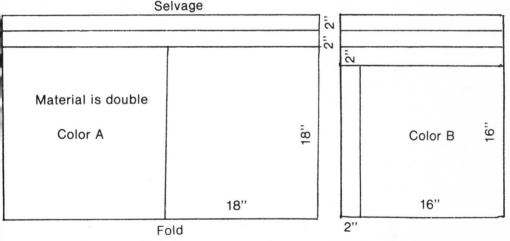

When you finish cutting all pieces, put everything in a plastic bag for later use. All you need to work with now is the once piece of contrasting material for the applique, and the 18" square for background material.

You are now ready to start your pillow.

1. Cut pattern on the eight-fold.
2. Applique design on background material.
3. Assemble pillow by placing muslin on bottom then filler, then applique on top, face up. Pin baste, then thread baste.

The quilting on your pillow will be the same technique used on the pot holder, just covering a larger space.

Give some thought to your quilting pattern. Remember the basic rules:

1. Place your hoop (if using one) in the center, and start quilting in the center.
2. Outline the appliqued material by quilting on the background material, following the design as closely as possible.
3. Dots have been placed on the pillow to suggest quilting lines. Feel free to vary.

PILLOW CLOSINGS

You may either use a zipper close, or an envelope close. The instructions on the outside of the zipper package are very precise and need no repeating here. Select a zipper about one inch shorter than your pillow, taking into account your seam lines. The zipper may be placed either in the middle of the back of the pillow, or at the bottom seam. The zipper should be put in before adding the binding.

For the envelope close, you will need a little extra material for the backing piece, since the back will be cut in two pieces, hemmed with a half inch hem, and overlapped one inch.

BINDING

Cut two strips of material 16." long 2" wide. Add to the sides of material, first pin basting then stitching on the machine. Cut two more strips 18" long. Add to top and bottom of pillow, stitching over two inch side bindings.

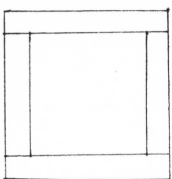

Fold the binding over to the back of the pillow, making a ¼" hem, and hand stitch completely around the pillow, enclosing the filler.

YOUR PILLOW APPLIQUE WILL LOOK LIKE THIS

Here are pillow patterns of the pineapple design originated by the author for this book and are the correct size for a 16" pillow without reducing or enlarging. For instructions in this book, we are going to make Pattern A Obviously Pattern B is more complicated than A, so take your choice.

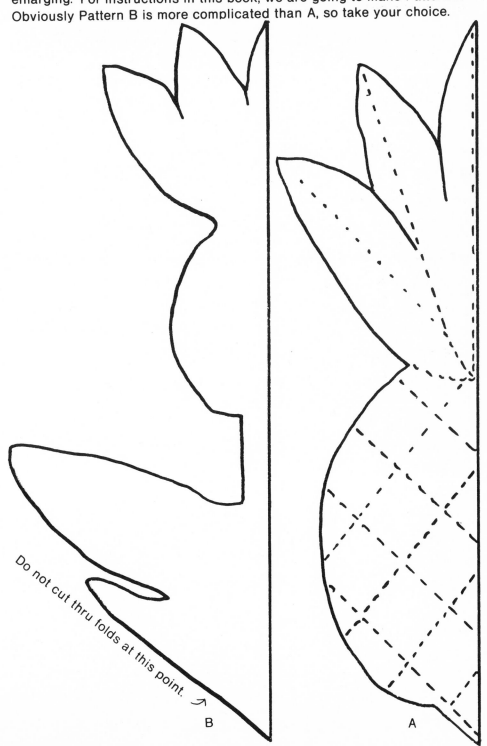

Do not cut thru folds at this point. ↗

B

A

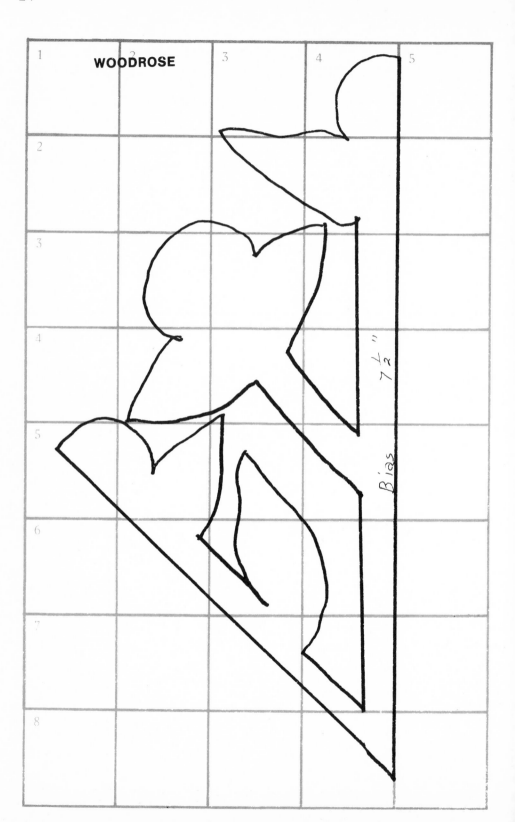

WOODROSE

Bias

$7\frac{1}{2}''$

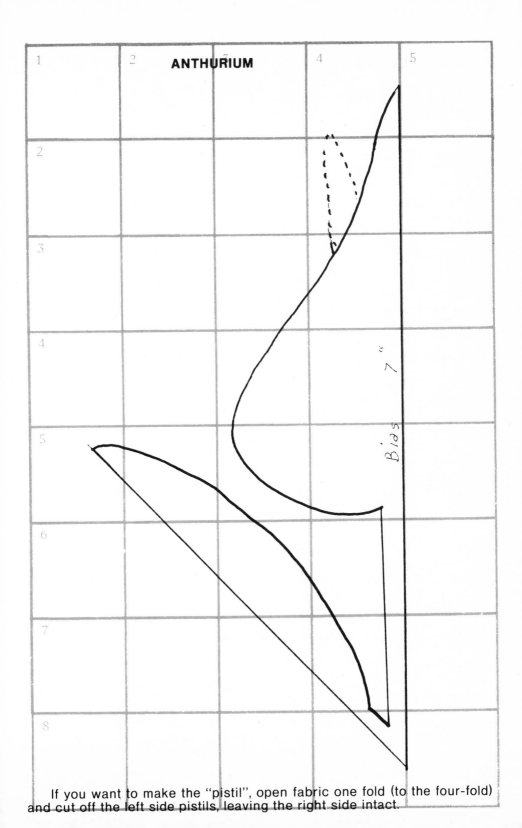

ANTHURIUM

Bias 7"

If you want to make the "pistil", open fabric one fold (to the four-fold) and cut off the left side pistils, leaving the right side intact.

HIBISCUS

Bias 8"

BREADFRUIT

Bias 8"

The theme "My Beloved Flag" has been repeated so many times, no book on Hawaiian quilting would be complete without at least one picture. This quilt made in 1915 by Mrs. Hoopii, is presented thru the courtesy of owner Mrs. Minerva L. Kalama of Maui. **KU'U HAE ALOHA** (My Beloved Flag)

CHAPTER 11 - THE HAWAIIAN QUILT

In the old days, not much attention was paid to the size of the quilt. Quilts were made for children and grandchildren, and usually not used as daily covers, but used for special occasions. Typical size of ancient quilts shown in past exhibits, would be 85 x 80, 84 x 83, 87 x 79, and such. None of the quilts exhibited in the 1973 Academy of Arts show ever reached 100 inches. The design was made to lay on top of the bed with no thought of touching the floor on all sides.

Today's quilts are usually designed for specific beds. Twin, double, queen or king. However, coverlets are still popular, and tutus are still making quilts for children.

There are two methods of making Hawaiian quilts. The block method, and the all-over-pattern. The block method of quilting is called Pohopoho in Hawaiian. For the block method, any of the pillow patterns may be incorporated into a quilt. The blocks may be joined together, or made into a larger quilt by using bands of material between the blocks. These can either be sewn by machine or by hand, but great care should be made to sew straight seams.

When making quilts, the following sizes may help:

Mattress	Bedspreads	Yardage
Twin 39 x 74	80 x 110	8
Dbl. 58 x 74	94 x 110	9
Queen 60 x 80	100 x 116	9
King 72 x 84	120 x 120	10

You will find that mattresses and bedspreads often vary by from 2 to 4 inches. Also, you may make a smaller quilt to fit your bed by using a "dust ruffle".

When cutting the pattern for an over all quilt, great care must be taken to make sure your folds are perfect and the pattern is pinned securely thru all 8 layers of the fabric. Keep material folded until ready to baste.

When using 9 yards of material, sew the 3 lengths of 3 yards each, as shown in this sketch.

If your material is such that it only requires two lengths, cut the one length in half, and assemble as in this sketch.

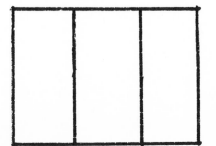

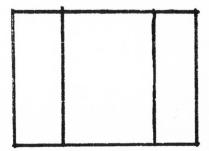

When ready to baste, lay the backing on the floor and secure corners and centers of edges with masking tape. Then add batting. If necessary to piece batting, do not overlay, but lay side by side and stitch the two together. Add appliqued front and again secure with masking tape. Pin baste center, then corners, and a few other pins where necessary. Some quilters use safety pins, saying it avoids getting scratched so much.

Start basting in the center and go to all corners, then straight out to center edges, then make a grid pattern as illustrated.

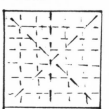

Remove pins as you thread baste, checking the back of your quilt carefully to avoid puckers.

YOU ARE NOW READY TO START QUILTING

1. Always start in center
2. Make short, even, stitches, preferably 5 or 6 to the inch.
3. Keep your contour lines even, marking material if necessary.

TO FINISH THE QUILT WITH BINDING

Cut strips of material the length of the quilt, and sew on the top side of the quilt, right sides together. Cut two more strips the width of the quilt PLUS enough to go across the two side bindings, and sew them on the quilt the same way. Press a hem on the binding and bring to the backing side, stitching by hand unless you're good at "Stitching in the ditch".

All the time you are working on your quilt it is wise to keep it on an old sheet. When you close up working for the day, merely bring the corners of the sheet together, tie, and everything is all nice and neat till your next quilting session.

1	2 **WOODROSE QUILT PATTERN**			5
Increase five or six times, using chart on page 10 as a guide.				
2				
3				
4			Bias 7¼"	
5				
6				
7				
8				

CHAPTER 12 - THE HAWAIIAN QUILTING SCENE - 1990

HAWAIIAN QUILTING IS ALIVE AND FLOURISHING

Hawaiian quilting IS enjoying a revival, and everyday in Hawaii, you'll find someone quilting. Many of the hotels have quilting demonstrations, and the many patterns as well as kits, currently on the market, make it easy for beginner to start. On all the Islands - magnificent quilts are to be seen. Some of the most popular places are listed on the following pages.

Alas, the former Maui Surf (now Westin Maui) listed in earlier editions of this book, no longer has a Kapa Room, or an Hawaiian Quilt Display. However, the quilts are all being carefully preserved "in storage". Who knows what the future will bring?

On the Big Island, page 35 reports about the wonderful quilts at the Mauna Kea Beach Hotel - but everyone should visit the Parker Ranch Visitor's Center Museum. Here you can see a flag quilt made for the Parker family in the early 1800s.

The Waianae Coast is loaded with magnificent quilters. Hannah Perry started the Waianae Library's collection of quilt patterns, which has now grown to over 400 - all available for you to trace. Quilting Master, Lydia Sharpe, in charge of the 1980 Waianae Quilt Festival, always has several quilt projects in the making, and always generous with sharing her expertise.

Wives at Hickam Air Force Base, meet weekly to quilt. Honolulu's Parks and Recreation give quilting lessons. Quilting IS alive and flourishing. Give it a try!

QUEEN EMMA'S SUMMER PALACE (Hanaiakamalama) 2913 Pali Highway, Honolulu, Hi. 595-3167

Too many people whiz up the Pali and fail to stop at this gem of a museum saturated in Royal history. Inherited by Emma Rooke at the age of 20, two year's later it became the Queen's Summer Palace when she married King Kamehameha the IV. Once nine acres, and now reduced to two, the white frame colonnaded building in its park like setting contains many pictures of royalty, magnificent furniture and china. There are several momentos of young Prince Albert, the first son born to a King in 50 years, only to die at the age of 4.

The Daughters of Hawaii, in charge of running the museum since 1915, have an excellent collection of quilts. However, there's only one on display. It's on Queen Emma's poster bed and is changed frequently, as that is better for the preservation of the quilts. They have done an excellent job of acquiring possessions of the royal family and restoring the palace to somewhat the grandeur it enjoyed in the 1870s.

Queen Emma was quite a seamstress, and two of her sewing machines are still on exhibit in the museum. On the back of the glass enclosed armoire containing Queen Emma's wedding dress, give special attention to the beautiful patchwork robe made by Queen Emma for the King. Velvets, silks and brocades, hardly any two alike, are meticulously stitched together with exacting feather stitches.

The No. 4 Nuuanu bus stops directly in front of the Palace, as does the 56 and 57 - Kailua and Kaneohe buses. There's plenty of room for rental car parking too. Open daily 9-4, the admission includes a guided tour, and well worth the trip.

CROWN AND WREATH from the Steven's collection. Orange leaves with a yellow crown are appliqued on a red background. Courtesy - Queen Emma's Summer Palace.

"Symbols of Royalty", showing the Hawaiian coat-of-arms, the kahili and maile leis, is just one of the 30 beautiful quilts so graciously exhibited at the Mauna Kea Beach Hotel.

MAUNA KEA BEACH HOTEL - Magnificent Quilts

The Mauna Kea Beach Hotel on the Big Island has long enjoyed the reputation of having the finest accommodations on the Orchid Isle. Corridors and court yards are loaded with museum quality objects of folk, primitive and antique art. Over a thousand of them.

When they decided to add Hawaiian quilts to their collection, Laurance S. Rockefeller commissioned Mealii Kalama to provide thirty 8-ft. square quilts to be used as wall tapestries in the hotel corridors. Mealii, one of Hawaii's foremost quilters, immediately accepted the challenge. With the assistance of her quilt making students, thirty quilts were blocked, battened and basted from designs cut free-form by Mrs. Kalama. After that, five experienced quilters from the Kawaiahao Church in Honolulu took over. They each expended over a 1000 hours per quilt, and tithed their portion of the commission proceeds. Each quilt is said to have over two million stitches.

These quilts, made of the finest percale, are color-coordinated to floral lithographs which adorn the guest rooms. The quilts, in all the shades of the rainbow, tell the story of Hawaii's natural environment: her flowers, fruits, leaves, landmarks and legends.

At first the quilts were hung directly on corridor walls, but between the elements and a little vandalism, it was necessary to rehang them in glass cases as they are today. These quilts are located along the corridors leading to the fifth and sixth floor guest rooms.

In tradition with the thoughtfulness and privacy Mauna Kea extends to its guests, these corridors are not open to the public. However, by special request it is usually possible for serious quilt enthusiasts to get permission to view these beautiful quilts. They are the most elaborate and beautiful collection of Hawaiian quilts on display in all Hawaii.

The Mauna Kea is a very special hotel and if it hasn't been in your experience, it should be. Aside from the many objects of art, the Mauna Kea is equally famous for its fine cuisine. While hotel rooms are always on the American plan, the dining rooms are open to the public. The buffet lunch is world famous and a gourmet's delight with table after table of fruits, salads, cheeses, cold cuts, hot entrees and desserts. They also offer a la carte service.

MISSION HOUSES MUSEUM - 553 S. King St., Honolulu 531-0481 9am-4pm

There's always a quilt on display on the spool bed which once belonged to Myra Chamberlain. Frequently there's another quilt or two in the Museum. A guided tour comes with the admission price and you'll certainly learn a lot from those informative docens. The first mission house was built in 1821 from material prefabbed in New England. The second was completed in 1823 from coral blocks, and housed the mission press, the first printing press in the Islands. The third house was built the same year.

The Mission Houses sponsor two very successful fairs each year; one in the Spring honoring King Kamehameha called "Fancy Faire"; the other in the Winter called "Christmas Fair" -- featuring special quilt displays.

HYATT REGENCY-WAIKIKI, 2525 Kalakaua Ave., Honolulu, Hi 96815
  The picture below is one of Mama Loke in days-gone-by. The quilt in the background is "White Ginger" and the one she is working on is "Lily."

HYATT REGENCY - WAIKIKI AT HEMMETER CENTER

The **HYATT REGENCY-WAIKIKI** does an excellent job of sharing Hawaiiana with visitors. Every day, some phase of arts and crafts are demonstrated. Fridays are very special, as they are in most of Hawaii. In fact Friday is usually referred to as "Aloha Friday" and business people are encouraged to wear muumuus and aloha shirts.

In 1983, they added a special Hyatt Hawaii Room (pictured below) where they share all phases of Hawaiian culture. You'll see beautiful quilts hanging on the walls, and there's always one in progress on a huge handmade frame. Some kits and quilting accessories are available, but the accent is on sharing with you. They are very happy to answer any questions, and they will even let you sit down and try a few stitches on your own.

The shop is located on the second floor behind the waterfall, and is open 9-5 Mon-Sat.

In 1969, Elizabeth (Betsy) Akana was given two Hawaiian quilts from her mother-in-law, that had been made for her husband upon his birth. Elizabeth was so impressed she decided to try a little quilting on her own, became more intrigued and started to take lessons from one of Hawaii's foremost quilters. That very same year, she formed EA OF HAWAII, a very successful venture that evolved into creating over 100 pillow patterns, many quilting patterns and interesting special projects. Elizabeth is truly a wonderful inspiration in the art of quilting. She travels to every major quilting show across the nation, and in 1983, sold EA of Hawaii in order to spend more time to spread awareness of the Hawaiian quilt, its uniqueness and the integral part it has played in Hawaiian history. She gives lectures, using color slides on ancient and contemporary quilts, to emphasize her points. Mrs. Akana can be reached at 46-334 Ikiiki St., Kaneohe, Hi 96844 (808) 247-5358. Her first full size quilt is pictured below.

EA OF HAWAII, P.O. Box 404, Lahaina, Maui, Hawaii 96767, (808) 661-0944

EA of Hawaii was established 23 years ago by Elizabeth Akana. In June of 1991 EA was purchased by Kathy and Larry Dunlap, to continue the traditions of Hawaiian quilting. EA has moved to a new home on the island of Maui and has a fresh new look.

EA of Hawaii continues to publish a quarterly newsletter—the Kapa Quarterly, which features articles on local quilters as well as exhibits and quilting projects in Hawaii. A year's subscription is $6.00 and includes a bonus pattern with each issue.

EA of Hawaii quilt and pillow patterns can be found in many stores throughout the islands as well as some mainland stores. A mail order catalog featuring patterns, wall hangings, pillow kits, quilting notions and books on Hawaiian quilting is published annually. Cost is $3.00.

KEPOLA U. KAKALIA, affectionately known as "Debbie," is one of Hawaii's most popular quilters. Kepola is truly a master of the arts. Her quilts and pillows have been on display in major quilt shows in the islands, as well as Mainland demonstrations and exhibits at the Mendocino County Museum and the DeYoung Museum in San Francisco.

Debbie occasionally teaches in the privacy of her home. She's also at the Bishop Museum on Monday and Friday, and at the Royal Hawaiian Shopping Center, Waikiki, on Tuesday and Thursday. She has a special talent for creating patterns and will create an exclusive pattern for you, on your material, using a theme you suggest, or a traditional Hawaiian theme. (808) 841-7286, 1595 Elua St., Honolulu, HI 96819.

Design by Poakalani
Copyright © 1973

Ulu

POAKALANI'S HAWAIIAN QUILTS

Born and raised in families whose Hawaiian quilting traditions were passed down from generation to generation, native Hawaiians John and Poakalani Serrao are considered master artisans and historians in the art of Hawaiian quilting and designing.

In 1972 John and Poakalani saw the art of Hawaiian quilting at its lowest interest and decided to continue their families legacy. Many who wanted to learn the art were unable to because of the size of the quilts and the lack of designs. Both John and Poakalani would introduce into the market 30 cushion size patterns for the beginner quilters and they would then become the first to design crib-size baby quilts. They would also be the first to introduce into the market Hawaiian Pillow cushion kits—pre-cut pillow kits ready to sew. John and Poakalani were instrumental in the revival of a dying art.

From 1972 to present, Poakalani and John Serrao have taught quilting and designing throughout Hawaii nationally and internationally. In 1988 they would formally teach weekly classes at the Queen Emma Summer Palace and the Royal Hawaiian Shopping Center.

Today they have over 78 cushion patterns, 12 crib size quilt designs and 12 quilt designs on the market. They have taught more than 1,000 students and designed more than 1,000 new quilt designs. Their students have learned to sew and quilt without tracing pencils. The students of Poakalani have become master quilters and most sought after in the state of Hawaii.

For John and Poakalani, Hawaiian quilting is not just a craft or hobby. It is an art, a tradition—the blending of the past and present on material. Hawaiian quilting is their tradition and their legacy to their culture, their families and their friends.

Poakalani and John Serrao can be reached at:

Poakalani Hawaiian Quilt Designs and Products
1720 Huna Street #106 • Honolulu, Hawaii 96817
Phone: (808) 524-0394 • (808) 521-1568 • Fax (808) 521-1626
email: cissy@lava.net • web site—http://www.poakalani.com

BISHOP MUSEUM, 1525 Bernice St., Honolulu, Hi 96817 (808) 847-3511
There are always some Hawaiian quilts on display in the Bishop Museum, on a rotating basis. By appointment, you may be taken into some of the storage vaults if you have a special interest in quilting. The Museum also offers quilting demonstrations on Mondays and Fridays in the Atherton Halau. Admission is included with your ticket to the museum, but if you want to stay 9 to 3 and take lessons, there is a $5.00 fee, not including material.

CHAPTER 13 - DRAWING FROM NATURE

This is the very popular **LAUA'E** found abundantly in Hawaii. The sketch below was actually traced from a leaf and reduced 62%. Notice how irregular the leaf is? Nature is like that. That is why, as earlier in the book, you were reminded it wasn't necessary to design or cut patterns with an engineer's exactness.

Here is a "Pillow Pattern" of the same fern. Notice how the space between leaflets has been filled in, requiring nothing but a slash. This is so when you turn under a minimum amount of appliqueing, your design will somewhat resemble the Laua'e leaf on the opposite page.

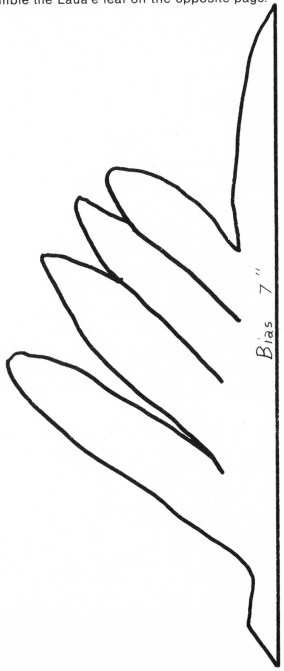

Bias 7"

HERE ARE SOME MORE HAWAIIAN FLOWERS FOR INSPIRATION

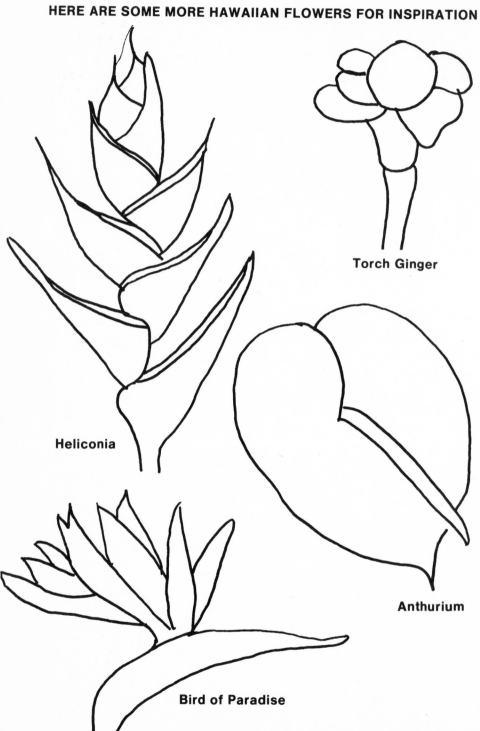

Torch Ginger

Heliconia

Anthurium

Bird of Paradise

BREADFRUIT LEAF

This is a tracing from a young Breadfruit tree leaf. At times they will have two or three leaflets on one side and three or four on another, growing to a maximum of four on each side.

AGAIN, you are encouraged to be as free and easy with your designs as mother nature is. Let your meticulous efforts be channeled into making small, even, stitches!

KUKUI LEAVES

These patterns are also traced from leaves. Although completely different in design, they are both from the same tree. The bottom leaf is more typical of the Kukui tree.

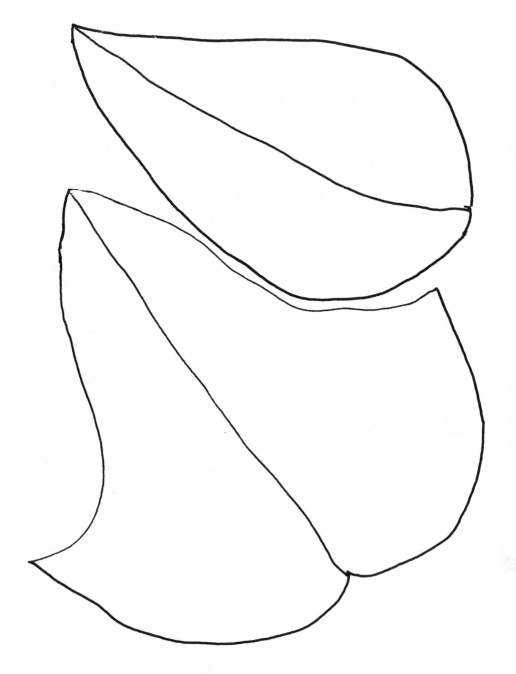

LIST OF ILLUSTRATIONS

Sketches Of Directions

Photos Of Quilts

Patterns

Miscellaneous

The following graph, designed in one inch grids, has been included to help you in creating your own designs, and for enlarging or reducing patterns. Make as many photocopies as you need.

1	2	3	4	5
2				
3				
4				
5				
6				
7				
8				